The Bible Storybook

The BIBLE STORYBOOK

By Gail Mahan Peterson

Illustrated by Fred Klemushin

Hallmark Children's Editions

Library of Congress Catalog Card Number: 73-90489.
Standard Book Number: 87529-382-4.

Contents

The First Days of God's World

There was a time when the whole world existed only in the mind of God. Through all of space, there was God alone until he created the heavens and earth.

But the heavens were dark and the earth was empty. So God said, "Let there be light!" And there was light, which God called "day." He separated the light from the darkness, which he called "night." And the daytime and darkness made up the first day of God's world.

Then God said, "Let the mist part to make sky above and oceans below." Then there was air and water in the world on the second day.

On the third day, God said, "Let the oceans gather together to make dry land." He called the land "earth" and the water "seas."

"Let the land bloom with every kind of grass and plant and fruit tree, with seeds inside them to make more of their kind." It happened as God commanded.

On the fourth day, God set the sun and the moon in the skies to make day and night, to make seasons upon the earth and to mark the days and years.

In the seas, God put every fish and water creature. In the air, he set in flight every form of bird. That was his work on the fifth day. And when God took a good look at all he had made, everything from wren to whale delighted the Lord God.

So God went on and filled the land with every beast that moves upon the earth, and then, on that sixth day, God made man to take care of his beloved world. At last, on the seventh day of the world, God rested, and he made his day of rest holy.

And so the world, set spinning by the love and power of God, began.

Noah and a New World

In the early days of the world, a morning came when the Lord looked out over his creation and was sorry he had ever made it.

The earth was fruitful. The skies were glorious in all shades of day and night. The world was alive with plants and animals perfectly formed in wonderful ways. But mankind, the creation that God loved most, greatly angered him. For God had given them the power and freedom to live as they chose, and they had chosen to turn from God's ways. Now, the perfect beauty of his world was spoiled by the ugly behavior of human beings.

One man alone still loved the Lord and showed his love by obedience to God's will. He was Noah. It was to Noah that God said, "I will destroy all that I have made, except for you and your family. You alone, Noah, give me joy."

The whole world was doomed! It was hard to believe! Yet Noah, full of faith in the Lord, did believe. He carried out God's instructions to build a boat, a huge ark, three stories high, 450 feet long, with a window at the top and a door in the side. Through that door Noah was to lead one pair – a male and a female – of every kind of animal.

Noah smiled as he worked, knowing that God could not completely destroy his creations. "Surely their form and nature still delight him! No, the Lord will save good seeds to furnish life for a new world washed clean of all evil."

And so, while all about him wicked people jeered and laughed, Noah and his sons, Shem, Ham, and Japheth, built the ark. Black clouds rumbled overhead, but the wicked went on laughing, not knowing they would never see the sun

again. Even thunder and lightning did not alarm them, nor the sight of Noah and his sons leading two of every kind of animal up the gangplank.

Wolves followed ducks, lions followed lambs, tigers followed deer. Aboard the ark, in stalls and nests and tanks made for them, there were clumsy rhinos and awkward giraffes, skunks and scorpions, guppies and roaches, hawks and doves – for it does take all kinds to make a world. Then, just as the door was bolted tight, the rains came.

Underground springs gushed forth. Rivers swelled. Lakes became seas. Seas became oceans. Still the water rose. For forty days and forty nights it rained and rained. Nowhere was there the sound of laughter now. All life perished except for those aboard the ark.

For one hundred and fifty days, the ark floated safely. Then, across the stillness God sent winds to blow on the water and dry it up. Slowly the waters receded.

Finally, the ark came to rest on the mountain called Ararat. Three months later, Noah could see the mountaintops. He sent out a dove, but the dove returned, for there

was still no land where it could light. A week later, Noah sent out the dove again. This time it returned with an olive branch to show Noah the water was nearly gone. When Noah sent it out once more, the dove did not return. It seemed that the world once more welcomed life. Yet Noah waited for God's orders. At last the Lord told him, "Take yourselves and every creature with you out upon the earth and multiply." Then Noah unbolted the door.

Grateful for the solid ground beneath his feet, Noah built an altar to God and gave many offerings in thanks. The Lord received them and made a promise to Noah, to his children and to all generations of people.

"I won't ever send another flood to destroy everything because of man," said God. "For proof, you can look to this sign." Across the heavens God stretched a mighty bow made of every color. How it gleamed and sparkled in the misty light of that first new day on the earth!

"As long as the earth remains," said God, "I, too, will see this sign and remember my promise. Now go. Be happy, be fruitful and be faithful to me."

A Son for Abraham

An old man called Abram stood gazing up into the night.
"How many stars do you see?" the Lord asked him.
"Far more than I could ever count, Lord!" said Abram.
"That is the number of descendants I will give to you and your wife Sarai," said God.
"But, Lord, we have no sons!" said Abram, laughing. "And I am an old man! Sarai is an old woman! How is it possible?"
"It is possible," God answered, "because I will bless you greatly. Give me your obedience, bear certain responsibilities, and I will give to you and yours a multitude of blessings, including this land Canaan. From now on, you will be called Abraham, which means 'father of nations'. Sarai will be Sarah. The generations to come out of you will be known as the children of God."

Not long afterwards, Abraham was sitting before his tent when three strangers approached. Quickly Abraham rose to welcome them. He sent word to have a good meal prepared. Sarah was to make fine cakes, while Abraham himself helped the strangers make themselves at home. He knew that the three men served God in some special way.
"Where is Sarah?" one of the men asked Abraham.
"There in the tent, Sir."
"Sarah will have a baby," said the man.
"What!" Sarah laughed out loud at the very thought. She was long past the age when women bear children.
"Why did Sarah laugh?" asked the stranger. "Is anything too hard for God? Abraham, you will have a son!"

As God promised, Sarah did give Abraham a son. "Name the boy Isaac, meaning 'laughter'!" said God.

Abraham and Sarah, both far into their old age, praised the Lord for his goodness to them. With a thankful heart, Abraham watched the boy grow up. Isaac was the blessing Abraham prized above all the wealth and honor that the Lord showered upon him.

"Surely nothing means more to you than that boy!" said Sarah, teasing her husband. And God decided to see if that were really true. He told Abraham, "Take Isaac up the mountain of Moriah and sacrifice him to me!"

Abraham obediently packed up for the three-day trip. Sorrow was his heaviest burden over the long, sad journey. He wondered why God wanted Isaac back, the precious child who was the gift of the Lord to Abraham's old age. How was Abraham to be the "father of nations" now? And to think that the boy's name meant "laughter."

Still, Abraham did not sway from the Lord's will. When they had arrived at the appointed spot, Isaac helped set the wood in place on an altar of stones. He turned to his father and asked, "But where is the offering?"

Abraham answered, "The Lord will provide for himself, Isaac." Then Abraham set his own son upon the altar. He raised his knife to slay the boy, but as the blade gleamed in the sunlight, an angel of God cried out from heaven.

"Abraham! Do not kill Isaac, for now the Lord knows who is still first in your heart, even before your beloved son."

Just then, a ram bleated nearby in the brush. Its horns were caught in the brambles, and the creature was held fast. "That is the offering the Lord asks of you," said the angel.

Oh, the joy in Abraham's heart now! He praised God with restored faith in the Lord's plans for him. Happily, Abraham and Isaac made their way home, dreaming of a wonderful future in the service of the Lord.

Joseph, the Slave Who Ruled Egypt

Isaac had a son named Jacob, also called Israel. Of the twelve sons that were born to Jacob, Joseph was his favorite. When Joseph walked among his brothers wearing the splendid coat that Jacob made him, his brothers seethed with jealousy. Then, when Joseph told them, "I dreamed you would one day bow down to me!" his brothers snatched him up and sold him to merchants on the way to Egypt.

Joseph grew up in Egypt as a slave. He was very capable, though, and was well respected — until he was thrown into prison under false charges. In prison with Joseph were two of Pharoah's own servants. One morning they awoke troubled by bad dreams. Joseph was able to tell the servants what their dreams meant.

He told Pharoah's butler, "Yours means you'll be back at work in three days. Please ask Pharoah to consider my case."

Indeed, the butler soon was serving Pharoah once more, but he forgot all about Joseph. It was two years later, when Pharoah himself had troubling dreams, that the butler remembered Joseph's unusual talent. At once Pharoah summoned Joseph and told him, "I dreamed of seven fat cows that were swallowed up by seven thin cows. Then I dreamed of seven full ears of corn swallowed up by seven bad ears. What does it all mean? No one can tell me!"

Joseph answered, "Both dreams foretell seven years of good harvest followed by seven years of famine. Put the wisest man you can find in charge of preparing for the hard times ahead."

Pharoah did just that. Amazed by Joseph's wisdom, which Joseph said God provided, Pharoah put the care of Egypt's harvest into the hands of Joseph and his God. No one but Pharoah was higher in rank.

Pharoah's dreams came true, but the storehouses held enough food to feed all the Egyptians. There was even enough left over to sell to other countries that were also stricken with famine.

From Canaan, Jacob sent his sons to buy food. Joseph recognized his brothers, but the men didn't know that the ruler they now bowed before was the brother they had sold into slavery. Joseph didn't tell them.

Into such a time Moses was born. Hoping to save his life, his mother laid Moses in a basket of bulrushes and set it afloat on the river. She prayed that the Egyptian princess who often came down to the river to bathe would find the beautiful baby and take pity on him.

Miriam, the sister of Moses, kept watch by the stream – and saw her mother's prayer answered! As the princess cradled the baby in her arms, Miriam stepped out of her hiding place.

"Shall I find a Hebrew woman to nurse the child for you?" asked the clever girl.

"Yes," said the princess, "and I will pay her for the service."

Of course, Miriam "found" her own mother! So Moses was returned to his own home, where he spent his first years under the protection of Pharoah's daughter – who even paid his mother to raise him for her!

When he was older, the princess sent for Moses, her adopted son, and had him brought into the palace. He was educated in the midst of great luxury, but Moses couldn't bear to watch the suffering of his people.

"I must help them," he told himself. But they would not accept his advice or leadership. Then when Moses in a fury killed an Egyptian for beating an Israelite, Pharoah became his enemy.

So it was that Moses left Pharoah's house, left Egypt and traveled to Midian, where he married and worked as a shepherd for his father-in-law. "Was I saved from the river and educated only for this?" he wondered.

Then one day, on the path before him, a bush suddenly caught fire. Moses saw that the bush burned but did not wither and die. The voice of God spoke to Moses from that burning bush.

"Moses, I'm sending you back to lead the people of Israel out of Egypt to a land I have prepared for them. This won't be easy for you. But I promise that when the time is right, every Egyptian and every Hebrew will know the power of the living God."

Moses returned to Egypt and, with his brother Aaron, showed Pharoah the amazing signs God had given him power to perform. But Pharoah was not impressed. Even when Moses made the river water turn to blood, Pharoah did not want to let the Hebrews go. The Lord cursed the Egyptians with seven plagues, but the stubborn Pharoah still refused.

Finally God told Moses to have every Hebrew family stain his front door with lamb's blood. Then God sent the angel of death to take the firstborn in every household in Egypt, passing over the doors that bore the sign of the Lord.

That night there was great mourning in Egypt, for in every family, even Pharoah's, there was one dead. At last, Pharoah in his grief *commanded* Moses to take the children of Israel out of Egypt.

They began their journey immediately, and the Lord went before them by day as a pillar of cloud and at night as a pillar of fire.

But Pharoah regretted his decision.

"Why should I free my own slaves?" he wondered. He sent six hundred chariots and his best men after them. The terrified Israelites found themselves trapped against a great sea with the Egyptians rushing toward them.

"Why have you brought us to destruction?" they cried to Moses.

"Be still; be patient," he answered. "Let the Lord show his power to fight for you!"

Then God told Moses, "Lift your rod and stretch your hand over the sea, and it will divide. The children of Israel will walk on dry land through the middle of the Red Sea!"

It was just as the Lord said. When the Israelites were safely across, the Egyptians pursued them across the same path. Once again Moses stretched out his hand, and the walls of water rushed together, swirling with God's power, over every one of Pharoah's chariots.

At first the Israelites stood in silent awe of God's might. Then how they rejoiced! From there, Moses led them forth, as the Lord instructed him. The way was long and hard, but Moses took care of God's people. He brought them out of bondage toward the land God had promised to them, the people descended from Abraham.

Gideon Leads God's Army

The children of Israel wandered forty hard years in the wilderness before God decided they were ready to receive the land he had promised them. At last, God caused the great city of Jericho to fall to their leader Joshua, and they entered the land of Canaan.

After a time, when the Israelites had long been settled there, they forgot their gratitude to the Lord and began to worship Baal, the false god of their neighbors. So the Lord God, who had brought them through such difficult times, did not protect the Israelites when vast armies rose up against them. For seven years, great hordes of Midianites helped themselves to whatever they wanted from the Israelites and destroyed their crops like grasshoppers. The Israelites could scarcely feed themselves. Then the day came when God moved to end their suffering. The Lord sent an angel to a young man named Gideon who was threshing out a little wheat for his poor family. The angel spoke to him. "Gideon, you are to lead your people against the enemies of Israel!"

"How can *I* do such a thing?" asked Gideon in disbelief, for he was nobody special, even in his own family. Gideon asked the angel for a sign from God to prove that the angel's message was real and really meant for him. He placed an offering upon a rock before the angel. At a touch of the angel's staff, smoke and fire burst out of the rock and consumed the offering. The angel vanished.

At first Gideon was terrified. But the peace of God filled him as he listened for God's instructions. Before God would help Gideon turn away the enemies of Israel, Gideon must

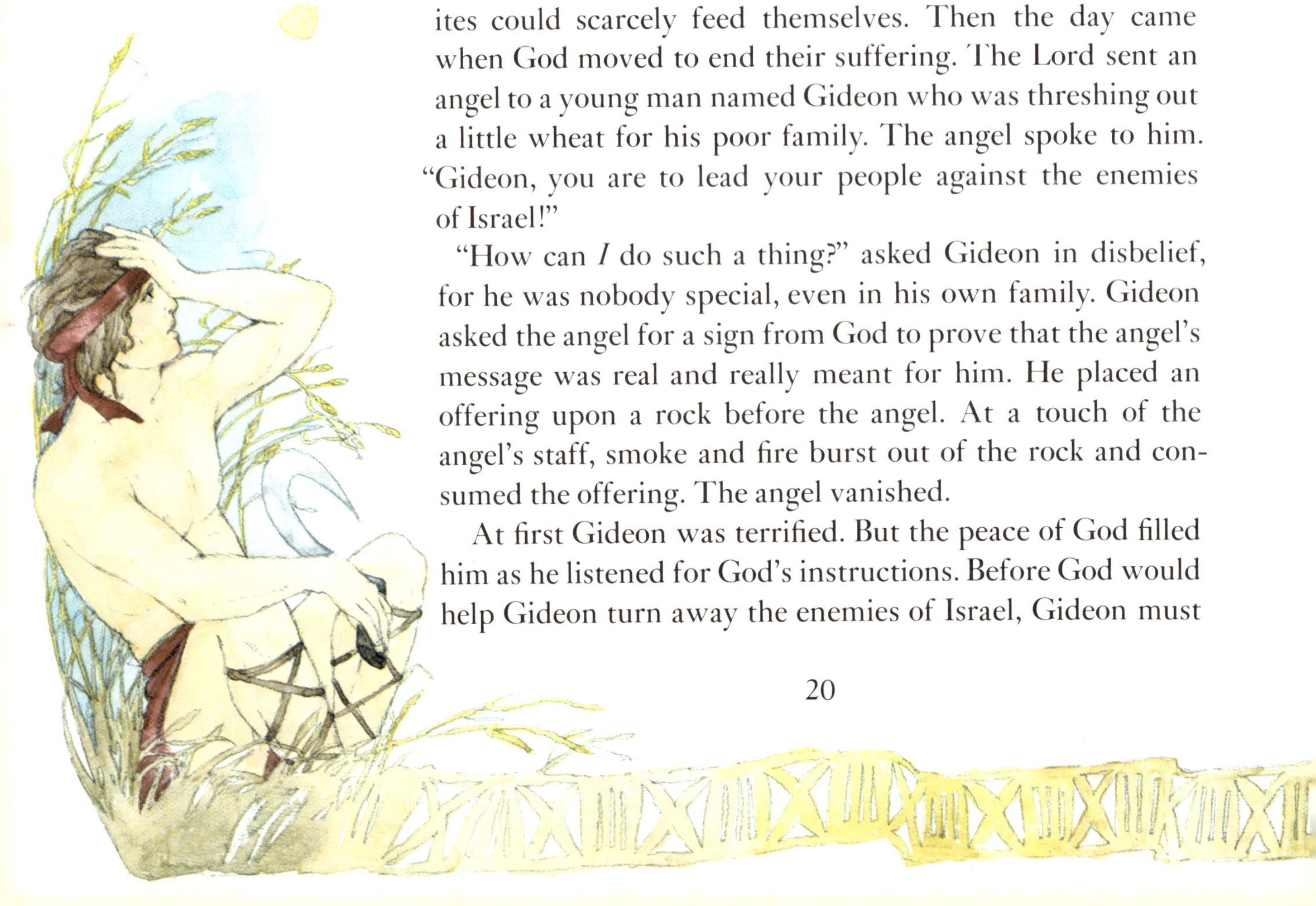

lead his people back to the worship of the one true God.

That night Gideon and a small band boldly destroyed the image of Baal and burned it on an altar to God. When the Israelites saw that the god Baal did not punish Gideon, they knew that he was no god at all, and they turned again to the God of their fathers. Now Gideon gathered his people as an army to fight the Midianites, but there were so many of them that Gideon wasn't sure of himself. Once again, he wondered about the orders God had given him.

"Lord, do you really mean to send *me*, Gideon, to save Israel against such a huge army?!"

"Certainly, Gideon!" answered the Lord. "In fact, *your* army is too big! If they should win, your men would surely believe they had done it by their own power. That's not how I want it. Send home the ones who are afraid."

Gideon sent them home – twenty-two thousand of them.

"Lord! I have only ten thousand now!"

"Still too many!" said the Lord. "You need only the strongest and the best of soldiers! Test them. Watch how they drink water from that pool."

Gideon saw that some of his men knelt down over the water, laying down their swords and shields to take a good drink. Others held on to their weapons and drank only what they could cup in one hand. Gideon knew which ones were the men for his army.

"But I have only three hundred, Lord!"

"They are enough," said God. "But if you're worried, take a friend and go down to thc Midianite camp tonight. Listen for a sign that will give you confidence in my plan."

Hiding outside the Midianite tents, which were as countless as grains of sand in the desert, Gideon heard one Midianite tell another, "I just dreamed that a barley cake rolled

into the camp and knocked our tent flat!"

The man's companion said, "That must have stood for the sword of Gideon, a man of Israel. God is going to give him a victory over us!"

That was sign enough for Gideon. He gathered his army of three hundred men. To each of them, Gideon gave a trumpet and a pitcher held over a light. In the night, he spread his men in a circle around the camp of the Midianites. All at one time, they blew their trumpets, broke the pitchers in their hands to let their lights shine, and they shouted together, "The sword of the Lord and Gideon!"

Startled awake in the middle of the night, the Midianites thought they were surrounded by what seemed to be thousands of Israelites. They were so confused that they began to fight with each other! The army of thousands fell into the hands of Gideon and God's great three hundred!

The Secret of Samson

"Tell me, Samson, what makes you so strong?"

A woman called Delilah pleaded with Samson, the Israelite, to tell her the secret of his amazing strength. Time after time, the Philistines, enemies of Israel, had tried to capture him. But Samson's strength was so great that once, with no more than the jawbone of a donkey, he slew a thousand of them.

Samson did have a secret, one the Philistines would pay well to know. If they knew what made him so strong, they might at last find a way to overpower him.

"Delilah, we'll each give you eleven hundred pieces of silver," said the Philistine commander, "to find out how we can capture this man!"

It happened that Samson loved Delilah, but Delilah loved the silver more than she loved Samson. She teased him, tricked him, begged and pleaded. "If you love me, you'll tell me the secret of your strength!"

Finally, Samson said, "If anyone binds me with seven green willow stems that have never been dried, I'll be as weak as any other man!"

While Philistine soldiers waited outside her chamber, Delilah tied up Samson while he slept, just as he had told her. Then she called out, "Samson! The Philistines are upon you!"

Samson broke through his bonds as if they were thread.

"Samson, you lied to me! If you loved me, you wouldn't keep important secrets from me!"

"If anyone binds me with new ropes that have never been used before," said Samson, "I'll be as weak as any other man." Again Delilah did as Samson told her. Again, she called out, "Samson! The Philistines are upon you!"

Samson burst the ropes like spiderwebs!

"Please, Samson! Please tell me the truth!" pleaded Delilah.

"Weave the locks of my hair into the cloth of your loom, and I'll be held fast like any other man."

While Samson slept, Delilah did so, and once more woke him saying, "Samson! The Philistines!"

This time Samson rushed out of bed carrying off the whole loom!

"How can you say you love me when you hold back such a wonderful secret!"

Delilah kept at him for days and days. Finally, weary of all her tears and tormenting, Samson let the precious secret out of his heart.

"Even before I was born, my parents promised to give me into the service of the Lord. I grew up having vowed never to cut my hair. If my hair were cut, all my strength would leave me," he told Delilah.

Sure of her reward now, Delilah rushed to the Philistines. One last time they waited outside while Delilah lulled Samson to sleep with his head in her lap. Then she called for a man to come and cut off the long locks of Samson's hair. When they were cut, she cried out, "Samson, you are surrounded!"

Without his strength, Samson fell at once into the hands of the Philistines. They put out his eyes, bound him with brass fetters and forced him to turn the wheel of the grindstone in the prison house. "Oh, Lord, is this your use for my life?" Samson moaned.

For a long time Samson labored in prison, long enough for his hair to grow slowly back, and for his strength to

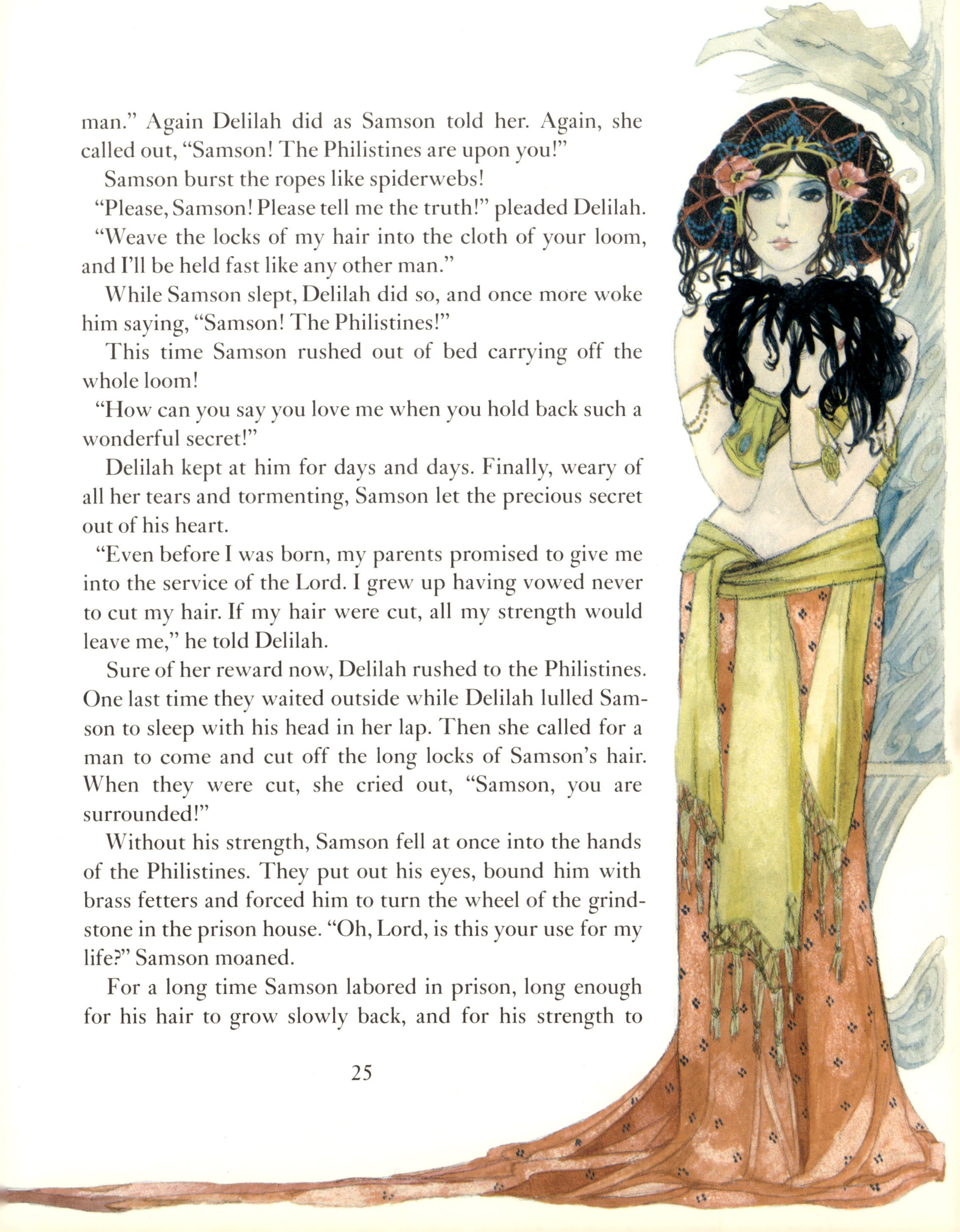

return without anyone's notice.

The Philistines were busy planning a great festival to celebrate the capture of Samson.

When the day arrived, they called, "Bring Samson out! Let him entertain us!" He was led by a boy into a huge temple filled with thousands of people. While the great mob of Philistines mocked him, Samson told the boy guiding his steps to lead him to the main pillars that supported the temple. Men and women surrounded him. All the Philistine leaders were there to watch. Three thousand more people looked down from the balconies. No one there knew that Samson, though sightless, had his strength back. But Samson knew, and now he understood how his capture and imprisonment served the Lord.

Bracing himself between the two pillars, Samson prayed, "Lord God, remember me, strengthen me this one last time so I can take revenge on the Philistines for my two eyes. Let me die in the task."

Then, with all his might, Samson pushed the pillars apart. They shook, swayed and crumbled. The roof caved in, the walls toppled, the temple fell – crushing the thousands of Philistines within it. Samson himself died, but by his death, he brought down more of God's enemies than he had ever overcome in all the days of his life.

Ruth's Journey to God

When a great famine spread over the land of Israel, a man named Elimelech, his wife Naomi, and their two sons moved to the country of Moab. There, Elimelech died, leaving Naomi with her sons and the Moabite women they had married, Orpah and Ruth.

After a time, Naomi's sons also died. Then the sad widow, Naomi, wanted to go home to Bethlehem. She knew the famine was over; so she set out from Moab with her two daughters-in-law.

On the way, though, Naomi decided that the young women would be happier in Moab, their own homeland. "Each of you return to your mother's house," she told Orpah and Ruth, although she loved them dearly.

Orpah cried and kissed Naomi good-bye, but Ruth clung to her. "Don't ask me to leave you," Ruth pleaded. "Where you go, I want to go, too. Wherever you stay, I will stay. Your people shall be my people, and your God, my God."

Naomi saw that Ruth loved her very much and was happy to have the young woman beside her on the journey to Bethlehem.

When they arrived in Bethlehem, it was the start of the barley harvest.

"Let me go in the fields and ask permission to gather whatever grain the reapers leave behind," said Ruth. It happened that Ruth went to the field owned by Boaz, a good man of Bethlehem and a relative of Naomi's husband.

"Who is that girl?" Boaz asked his servant in charge of the reapers.

"That's the girl from Moab who came back with Naomi. I said she could glean in your fields."

Boaz went to Ruth and said, "My dear, don't go to glean in any other fields but mine. And whenever you're thirsty, drink from my water jars."

Ruth was amazed by his kindness to her. "I am a stranger! Why should you bother with me?"

"I've heard how you stayed by Naomi and came here far from your own people. May the Lord repay your good deeds!

day. Tall and strong, David also served as King Saul's armor-bearer until he was called home to help his father when his older brothers joined Saul's army.

Israel was at war with the nation of Philistines. One morning, a Philistine warrior stepped forward and bellowed, "Send one man to fight me! Let our combat decide the victory between our two armies!"

He was Goliath, a giant over nine feet tall. For forty days he challenged the Israelites, but no one dared to fight him.

Then David came into camp bringing supplies to his brothers. He heard Goliath's arrogant challenge. David asked, "Who is he to defy God's army? I will take him on!"

The Israelites laughed. His own brothers mocked him. But word reached Saul that David meant what he said.

"How can a peaceful lad like you overcome a giant trained in war all his life?" Saul asked David.

David told Saul how the Lord was with him in all things, how he had slain both a bear and a lion with no help but God's.

"But a giant?" asked Saul. "Well, take my spear and shield, and the Lord go with you!"

"Please, may I take my own weapons? I'm not used to yours."

Quickly David went out alone to face Goliath. He carried only a shepherd's staff and a slingshot.

The giant was furious. "What am I, a dog, that you send a boy to beat me with a stick? Hah!" roared Goliath. "I will feed him to the birds!"

"No, Goliath," said David. "You come to me with a sword and a spear, but I come to you with the Lord God of Israel. Today he has delivered the Philistines to the Israelites. By my hand, God will slay you so the world will know the living God of Israel!"

Outraged, the giant lunged at David. David slipped a stone into his sling, took aim and shot it. Suddenly, Goliath fell back and crashed to the ground. The stone was buried deep in his forehead. Then David leaped for Goliath's sword and cut off the giant's head so that the Philistines could see their fierce warrior was really dead. Horrified, the Philistines scattered, chased to their own gates by Saul's army.

The joyful Israelites sang David's praises. The shepherd boy who had slain a giant would one day be their king – a king as great in battle against God's foes as he was gifted in song and the ways of peace.

Jonah Does His Job

God spoke to Jonah, the son of Amittai. "I want you to go to the great city of Nineveh and tell the people there how their evil ways offend me."

Jonah knew what a terrible place Nineveh was, so instead of obeying God, he ran away to Joppa, where he boarded a ship bound for Tarshish.

"Let Nineveh roast for its sins!" he thought to himself with no pity whatever.

When the ship was out on the seas, wind followed wind until the blackest of storms swirled around the ship and its crew. All the sailors cried out to their gods for mercy, all but Jonah, who was sound asleep, as if he could hide in dreams from God's will.

"Jonah!" the captain called to him. "Wake up! Don't you care about our lives? Pray to your god, too, for our safety!"

The sailors drew straws, believing they could find out by whoever drew the shortest straw, which one of them was causing his god to bring on such a storm. Jonah drew the short straw. "I worship Jehovah, the almighty God of heaven who made the seas and the land. Because of me, God has sent this storm. I've run away from him," Jonah admitted.

"What will we do with you?" cried the sailors. "Why should we all die because of the quarrel between you and your God?"

"Throw me overboard, and the storm will subside," said Jonah. "It's all right. I deserve to die."

The sailors couldn't bring themselves to do that until they saw there was no other hope for them. Finally they hurled Jonah into the sea. Instantly the wind and the waves were still.

The men were astounded. "What a mighty God is Jonah's!" they cried to each other. As their ship moved through calm waters, the sailors sacrificed to God and made promises to serve and worship only him.

Under the waves, Jonah expected to die. But the Lord sent a great fish to swallow him. Inside the fish, Jonah found he was still alive.

"Oh, Lord, you have saved me! You heard the cry of my miserable soul and came to me, even at the last desperate

moment! How can I thank you?"

Jonah spent three days and nights in the belly of the fish. Then God had the great fish throw him up on the land.

"Now then, Jonah," said the Lord, "I believe we were discussing Nineveh. Go there and tell the people what I command you to."

It was a three-day journey to Nineveh. This time, Jonah made the long trip obediently. He went about the city crying, "In forty days God will destroy Nineveh!"

The people were horrified. They believed the word of God through Jonah. Every one of them, from beggar to king, fasted, repented and cried loudly to God. And God forgave Nineveh. He changed his mind and did not destroy the city after all.

That made Jonah furious! "I knew you'd do that!" he raged. "I know how merciful and forgiving you are! How can I ever face those people after what I've told them?"

Jonah made some shelter for himself on a hillside beyond the city, where he could watch what God might yet do to Nineveh.

It was very hot. God made a gourd vine grow up to shade Jonah, and Jonah was very grateful for it. But God also sent a worm that ate the vine and made it wither away within a day. And God made the sun beat down hard on Jonah's head until he felt so sick he wished he were dead.

"So you miss the gourd vine, Jonah?" asked God. "You cry for such a simple thing – which you put no effort into making! Well, if that vine is so precious to you, think how much more precious to me is a great city of 120,000 men, women and innocent children, all of which I created – not to mention their cattle! Think, Jonah! Shall I not save them in their sins as I saved you?"

Esther the Queen

Ahasuerus, a king who ruled over one hundred and twenty-seven provinces from Judea to Ethiopia, was looking for a queen. Of all the women brought to him, from all parts of his empire, the girl he most desired was Esther. She lived with her uncle Mordecai, who had come from Jerusalem and now lived and worked right there in the king's palace. Mordecai instructed Esther to keep it a secret from everyone at the palace that she was a Jewess.

One day, after Esther was crowned queen, Mordecai overheard two of the king's chamberlains plotting against Ahasuerus. Mordecai quickly sent word to Esther, and when the king learned the truth of Mordecai's story, he had the two chamberlains slain and gave Mordecai credit for saving his life.

After that time, the king placed a rich and arrogant man called Haman over all the princes in the realm. By the king's order, everyone was to bow before him.

"I bow only to God," said Mordecai. He would not bow down to Haman.

"So the Jews will not respect me!" thought Haman. "Then I will take care of the Jews!"

"King Ahasuerus," said Haman, "there is a certain group

of people living in various parts of your kingdom who keep different laws from yours. Why should you tolerate their disobedience to your commands? I'll pay you a fortune for the pleasure of extinguishing them!"

"I trust your judgment," said the king. "You can keep your money and do as you see fit." He gave Haman his own ring to seal the orders that Haman sent to the governors of all provinces, saying that the Jews should all be destroyed on a certain day in the following year.

When Mordecai learned of Haman's orders, he put on sackcloth and ashes, the clothes of mourning and repentance, and went through the royal city crying and wailing. Esther's servants told her about him. She sent one to ask what troubled him.

Her servant returned with a copy of Haman's decree and brought with it a message from Mordecai pleading for Esther to go to the king and defend her people.

"But no one can go before the king without being summoned!" cried Esther. "By law, the penalty is death. And the king hasn't called for me in a long time." She sent that message to Mordecai.

Mordecai answered, "Think, Esther! Perhaps it's just for this purpose, to save your people, that you've been placed by God in such a position!"

Esther trembled in fear for her life, but she worried even more for the lives of Mordecai and her people.

"Gather all the Jews in the city," she told Mordecai through her servant. "Have them pray and fast for me, not eating or drinking for three days and nights, as my servants and I shall do. Then I will go to the king, although it's against the law, and if I perish, I perish."

On the third day, Esther put on her most beautiful robes

and stepped quietly into the king's inner court. From his throne, the king saw Esther. Because he loved her very much, he held out his golden scepter to her, the sign that her life was to be spared.

"What would you like, Queen Esther?" said the king. "I will grant your wish, even if it's for half the kingdom!"

"If it pleases your Highness," said Esther, "come, with Haman, to a banquet that I have prepared for you. Then I will tell you my wish."

They did, and over the wine, the king again said, "Queen Esther, tell me your desire! So I can grant it! Even if you'd like half my kingdom!"

Then Esther told him, "Oh, King Ahasuerus, I desire only that you'll again spare my life and the lives of all my people. For a decree has been sent out by which we are all doomed to die!" Not knowing that Esther was one of the "people" Haman meant to destroy, the king was astonished. "Who made such a decree? Who dares to presume this authority?"

Esther answered, "Haman." Startled, Haman jumped from the table.

One of the chamberlains spoke up and said, "Look out there at the gallows which Haman has made for Mordecai, the man who once spoke so well for the king through Queen Esther!"

"Hang Haman on it," ordered the king. That very day, King Ahasuerus gave Haman's house and vast riches to Esther and sent out new orders sparing the Jews. He summoned Mordecai and gave him the ring he had once given Haman, then sent him out wearing royal robes and a crown. Everyone rejoiced for him.

Then, throughout the kingdom, the Jews had happiness and honor among all the people.

Daniel in the Lions' Den

When the city of Jerusalem was conquered and destroyed by Nebuchadnezzar, king of Babylon, a boy named Daniel was one of the captives carried away. However, in Babylon, he and three of his friends – Shadrach, Meshach and Abednego – were picked out to be educated by scholars at the king's court because they were such extraordinary young men.

Daniel grew up to be the wisest man in the kingdom. Even when Babylon itself fell under the rule of Darius the Mede and became part of the empire of Persia, Daniel was still paid supreme respect. In fact, when King Darius set one hundred and twenty princes to rule over his kingdom and named three presidents above them, he made Daniel the president with top authority over all the other rulers. The most powerful men in the land had to answer to Daniel. How they wished they could find even one flaw in his brilliance to rob Daniel of the king's trust and affection for him.

Daniel was an excellent ruler, but one who always put the laws of God before the laws of the kingdom. He praised the Lord with reverence he would show no man. So the jealous

leaders decided to use Daniel's worship of God to prove him disloyal to the king.

They went to King Darius and said, "To enhance your power, Sire, why not make a royal decree, one that can't be changed, according to the laws of the Medes and Persians, that whoever requests anything of anyone but you for thirty days must be thrown to the lions!"

The vain king signed their idea into law. But when those rulers came back and reported to him that Daniel continued to bow down to the God of Jerusalem, Darius was miserably sorry he had made the law because he loved Daniel.

"I can't change the law!" he cried to himself. "Now I must do what it decrees!"

Darius had Daniel thrown into the den of lions, but then he called down to him, "Daniel, I hope the God you trust so much will save you now!"

All that night Darius fasted and paced the floor without sleeping. Perhaps he remembered the story of King Nebuchadnezzar – how he had thrown Shadrach, Meshach and Abednego into a fiery furnace because they would not bow down to his golden calf. The flames were so hot they killed the men tending the furnace, yet the three young Israelites stepped out of the flames completely unharmed because their God had protected them.

In the morning, Darius rushed to see what had become of Daniel. The lions yawned like well-fed cats instead of fierce and hungry beasts. In their midst, without a scratch, stood Daniel.

"I'm all right!" he called to the king. "Just as God sent his angel to shield my friends in Nebuchadnezzar's fiery furnace, he has sent his angel to close the lions' mouths! I've been saved so you could see the power of my loving God!"

Darius was amazed and happy beyond words. He had Daniel brought up out of the lions' den, and in his place had the men thrown to the lions who had schemed against Daniel.

This time the lions behaved like lions, and Daniel's accusers perished. Then King Darius made a new decree to all people and nations, and in all languages.

"Peace to you forever! I now command that in every part of the kingdom, everyone shall revere the God of Daniel! For his God is the living, unchanging God whose kingdom shall never be destroyed and whose power shall never end! See how he delivers his people! Saves them from harm! And works great miracles in heaven and earth! He has saved Daniel from the lions, praise the Lord God!"

Set in Janson,
a typeface designed by Nicholas Kis
in Amsterdam around 1690.
Printed on Hallmark Eggshell Book paper.
Book design by Myron McVay.